A Leeds Life

Charles Brears, Collier to Shopkeeper
1854 - 1938

Peter Brears

ISBN 978-1-904446-45-3

British Library Cataloguing in Publication Data
Peter Brears 2013
A Leeds Life
Charles Brears, Collier to Shopkeeper, 1854-1938

Printed and published by
Quacks Books
Petergate
York YO1 7HU

Contents

Introduction

Back in the 1940s, when there was a severe housing shortage throughout England, I lived with my mother and father at his parents' home at 75 Longthorpe Lane, Thorpe, mid-way between Leeds and Wakefield in the West Riding of Yorkshire. Being detached, and on top of the ridge separating the broad Aire and Calder valleys, it was always a cold and windy spot, never more so than in the spring of 1947, when I remember the snow being six or seven feet deep for weeks. Only the kitchen fire burned every day in the black-leaded and gleaming chrome-fitted Yorkshire range. While the rest of the house remained sub-Arctic, here all was warm, as every dish for every meal, every item of bread or cake, and the firebricks which, wrapped in flannel, served as our hot-water bottles, were respectively boiled, baked or heated by the glowing coal fire. After the evening meal – always 'Tea', rather than the more polite 'Dinner', chairs were drawn up around the fire, the lights were turned off to save electricity, and everyone talked together until supper. This usually comprised bread, cheese and the strongest of onions, with tea, or perhaps 'Horlicks'.

Much of the conversation was about earlier times, and earlier generations. As it went on, the family bible, which had entries going back to the late eighteenth century, might be brought out to check dates and relationships. Objects might appear too, including photographs, inscribed books, etc., inherited handtools and equipment which still remained in regular use. There was nothing unusual in this; it is what most working-class families did most evenings before television became more common from the mid 1950s. It not only passed the time, while probably sewing, darning, knitting string dishcloths, or making rag rugs were carried out, but it drew the family together and gave them a sense of identity, with themselves, their ancestors, and their localities. Knowing where you came from was not a bad foundation for starting out on life. Like many others, I had absorbed this knowledge quite unconsciously, and only many years later realised how useful it had been in shaping my own interests and career.

The kind of family life just described has now largely disappeared. Many children live in homes which are deserted for most of the day, where meals are bought in and taken individually rather than communally, and evenings are spent in front of an impersonal television or computer screen, and/or wearing headphones/earpieces to exclude real life as much as possible. Partly to show how much personal information used to be passed on orally from one generation to another, and partly to organise a wealth of different memories and ephemera into a meaningful whole, I thought it would be worthwhile to set down my family's story as it developed in the nineteenth and early twentieth centuries. Between 1800 and 1914 Britain led the world in a series of social and industrial developments of unprecedented magnitude. In retrospect, the fortunes of every working family may be seen to have shared many common experiences, each reflecting these changes in microcosm.

Perhaps the greatest period of progress took place in the late Victorian and Edwardian periods, with the increasing move of rural populations into the mushrooming industrial cities, the development of universal education, and the expansion of various religious and social organisations dedicated to the improvement of working class life. My great grandfather Charles Brears (1854-1938) lived all his life in south Leeds. Although I never met him, I grew up using his furniture, reading his books, looking at his photographs, and playing with some of the toys he had bought for his children. I had also heard much about his life during my childhood fireside conversations. He therefore provided an ideal subject around which to gather and arrange an otherwise random collection of miscellaneous memories and artefacts. What emerges is a useful, revealing and, hopefully, interesting picture of an ordinary life, illustrated by insights into forgotten local industries, domestic interiors, social events and other everyday matters.

When writing on any historical matter, it is usual for the author to consult every available document and record before setting pen to paper. Here, however, virtually no external research has been undertaken. This has been a deliberate policy, not because further information would not be forthcoming, but because this book is intended to show just how much unique knowledge of the past may be accumulated in the memories and artefacts of any ordinary family.

This is the story of someone who was born to relatively poor, illiterate working parents, started his working life as a collier, set up his own small business, took an active part in the life of his community, and enabled his son to enter professional life. In all of these activities he shared the self-improving opportunities available to thousands of working-class people in late Victorian England, as economic growth fostered personal development and prosperity. Along with many others, his much-used and favourite expression was that of 'Procrastination is the thief of time!' - in other words 'Keep busy!' and pursue the course plotted in Samuel Smiles' work on self-improvement.

The Family

Charles Brears' family originated around the Isle of Axholm close to the Yorkshire-Lincolnshire border in the former West Riding. They had farmed here throughout the eighteenth century, the wills of William and Robert Breares recording them as yeomen farmers at Skelbrook in 1703 and 1709, for example. By 1800 sixty-year old John Breares and his wife Hannah, aged sixty three, were farming in the parish of Thorne. They had married in the late 1760s and had a large family of seven boys and two girls all born between 1768 and 1790. Thomas Breares, the fourth son, was born in 1777, and later married Mary Brown, daughter of another farming family in Thorne. Many years later, their family bible was filled with records of both their families; 'These are Thos. Breares Brothers & Sisters Names and ages. David & James Breares Too brothers died [i.e. did] this writting April 23, 1833'. Their spelling was not too good, but they were apparently proud to boast of their literacy. Thomas and Mary had a family of three boys and three girls between 1808 and 1832. They probably all lived together up to the early 1840s, but the death of the eldest son Charles in 1838, and his father Thomas in 1839, combined with the increasingly harsh economic climate as Britain entered the 'Hungry Forties', now made the other sons move out to find work elsewhere.

Thomas, the second son, decided that there was no future in agriculture, and so, on 24th March, 1842, aged twenty four, he travelled to Newark and joined the army. As No. 2094, Private Brears of Her Majesty's 64th Regiment of Foot, he spent the next twenty two and a half years as a soldier. For more than half of this time he served in India, his medals including those of the Persian Campaign of 1856-7, the Indian Mutiny of 1857-8, and also others for Long Service and Good Conduct. On 10th September, 1863, when he was forty eight, he obtained his discharge at Aldershot with a pension of tenpence halfpenny (c.4.5p) a day. He then intended to live in Wakefield, only a few miles from his younger brother David's family who were then

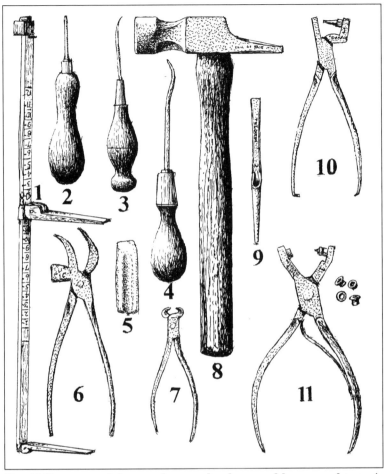

David Brears used these tools to make shoes and boots, and to train his son and grandson the skills they needed to repair their own and their families' footwear.

1.	Counter stick	7.	Cutting nippers
2.	Clicker's awl	8.	Shoe hammer
3.	Sewing awl	9.	Point punch no. 2
4.	Heel awl	10.	Punch plier
5.	Wax for thread	11.	Eyelet plier & eyelets
6.	Lasting pincers		

living in Rothwell. After eight years in civilian life, he decided to return to his military roots, and so became a Chelsea Pensioner, living in the Royal Hospital from 1st October 1871, up to the time of his death aged 72 on 15th February, 1887.

David, the youngest son, had been trained as a cordwainer, or shoemaker, and decided there would be more chance of finding work if he moved from a farming area to one where industry was expanding. It is not known why he chose Rothwell, but it was to this small market town of 3000 people, five miles south east of Leeds, that he moved in the mid 1840s. Coal-mining was the main local industry, along with quarrying, ropemaking and matchmaking. Here he probably started work as a journeyman cordwainer, that is an apprentice-trained craftsman working for an independent master, a trade he followed for the rest of his life.

On the 7th of March, 1848, David married Eliza Moor at Rothwell Parish Church. Both were illiterate, and instead of signing the register, they made their mark with a cross. The certificate states that she had been born in Featherstone, a mining village between Wakefield and Pontefract, but she must have moved to Rothwell in her early childhood for she remembered being trained at a lace school near Chatham House on Oulton Lane, just to the north-east of its junction with Gillett Lane. The school occupied the second storey attic room at the west end of the terrace, its Yorkshire sliding sash window being pointed out to me by my grandfather.

Coal mining and lacemaking appear to be an unlikely combination, but in fact they both complemented each other to meet the needs of the community. Mining was a constantly dangerous and crippling industry. When aged 20 a collier averaged 40% more sickness than an agricultural worker, this rising to 78% by the time he was forty. Similarly his life expectancy was only 27, in contrast to the others' 43. In such circumstances, and in the days of large families, it was essential for wives and mothers to have an alternative source of regular income. Up until the 1841 Act of Parliament women were still

Eliza Brears (1828 – 1918)
'The Last of the Rothwell Lace-makers'.

employed underground. Frequently they worked as hurriers, a chain passing around their waists and between their legs enabling them to drag corves or baskets of coal from the coalface to the pit bottom, crawling on hands and knees along the low-roofed galleries. A family tradition recorded that one of Eliza's sisters worked in this way up to 1841. Even after the Act many local women still worked at the pit banks, riddling the coal and loading it on to carts.

The Rothwell lace industry had provided a welcome alternative female occupation from around 1800. In 1812 young girls were being given year-long apprenticeships in lace schools run by Suzy Cave, Sally Holt, Fanny Bilsbrough and Hannah Gill. Using linen thread wound on wood or bone bobbins and parchment patterns mounted on 'round-ended oblong' cushions, they were taught the various patterns called half-frill and three-quarters frill, presumably named after the width in inches. Other patterns were called simple bell, double ox-eye, toad-face, scallop with head in, barleycorn, three stalks, running river, princess feather, and diamond. As they worked, the girls 'counted their pieces backwards, repeated things', or sang, to produce a sort of humming confusion. Having completed their course, each girl was presented with her own equipment or 'tackling' and a new print dress. She could then work from home. The lace sold for between 4d (2p) and 9s (45p) a yard, depending on its width and intricacy, George Wilsdon of Oulton being the local lace dealer in 1848. Cash sales were comparatively rare however, except when the local gentry bought a quantity to support the lacemakers. Instead, it was customary for hawkers or pedlars of drapery to exchange goods, especially items of clothing, for the lace. One of these, Thomas Wilson, was still remembered in the 1870s.

In the mid-late nineteenth century the Rothwell lace industry went into decline, since it could not compete with the machine-made lace of the Nottingham factories. Eliza was apparently one of the last apprentice-trained lacemakers here and, since she continued to work up to the time of her death on 13th May, 1918, aged 90, she enjoyed the celebrity of being 'The last of the Rothwell Lacemakers'. It was in this role, sat behind her pillow, that she was photographed by Charles Sidebottom of 25 Royds Lane, Rothwell, almost at the end of her long life.

Some time in the 1890s she sent lengths of at least four different patterns of her lace to her son Charles' wife and sisters-in-law, Mary Ann, Ellen and Elizabeth Boucher of Ripley, near Harrogate, where they were kept in an envelope noted with their history, until the youngest of them died in 1954, after which they

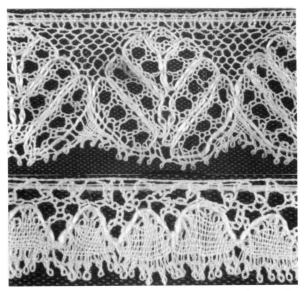

Rothwell lace worked by Eliza Brears in the 1890s.

Each design of Rothwell lace was given a local name, such as 'simple bell' or 'toad-face', but unfortunately these can no longer be linked to these unique surviving samples.

came into my care. They therefore remain the only provenanced examples of Rothwell lace. In 2002 I submitted them to Santina M. Levery, the country's leading authority on the subject, who confirmed that they were all made with cotton ground threads (2 unspun 5 ply) and thick linen gimp thread (2 unspun 2 ply). Three were worked using the widespread Bucks-point, and the fourth in torchon lacework.

The combination of David's shoemaking and Eliza's lacemaking were insufficient to maintain a separate household, and so the couple lived with Eliza's father, William Handforth, who worked as a coal miner. His house at 48 Town Street (later re-named Commercial Street) was also occupied by his wife Ann, daughter Sarah Jane, and 12 year-old son Aaron, probably already in the mines. Within a year David and Eliza had started their family, seven children being born over the next 13 years;

Thomas (13/12/1849 – 10/12/1932), left home in the 1860s, later working as a gardener, marrying and having three children.

Eliza Lidster (3/9/1850 -), died in infancy.

Mary (12/8/1851 – 30/4/1931), lived most of her life in West Cumbria.

Charles (16/8/1854 – 24/9/1938), the subject of this book.

William (20/7/1857 - ?), continued as a pupil/teacher at Holy Trinity School, Rothwell. When he left to become headmaster at St.Ives Church of England School, Leadgate, County Durham, he was presented with a fine brass-bound burr-walnut writing slope inscribed 'PRESENTED to William Brears by the Teachers and Scholars of Rothwell Parish Church Schools, Jan.y. 28Th 1876.'

Ann Eliza (17/6/1860 - ?), married William Jackson of Muncaster in 1885, her children and grandchildren living on the Castle estate through to 1986.

David (3/12/1862 – 22/8/1864)

By 1861 David, Eliza and their family had moved to 27 Town Street, by 1871 to 24 Town Street, and by 1891 to 4 Smithson Street, at the junction of Marsh Street with Royds Lane.

Early Life & Interests

By the time that Charles was 17 he had left school and followed his grandfather and uncle down the pit. As one of seven children born to poor and illiterate working parents, it should have been expected for him to remain in the mines for the rest of his life. However, there were a number of relatively new facilities in town for anyone interested in improving their personal prospects. In 1869 the new Rothwell Mechanics Institute opened its doors for educational and social activities, for example, Charles not only attending its classes, but serving as its honorary librarian from his early twenties.

His primary education at the Church Schools had already taught him to read, and to write in a very neat and elegant copper-plate script. As librarian, he had ready access to a wide range of books, which fostered his interest in literature. Later he became a subscriber to periodicals such as *The Quiver* or *The Strand Magazine*, which he had bound up year after year. The latter included the original illustrated versions of Conan Doyle's stories of Sherlock Holmes, which I found still thrilling to read sixty years later. In addition, he bought volumes of poetry, both by established English poets, and by local dialect writers, John Hartley's *Yorkshire Ditties* of 1868 being a particular favourite, especially for recitations. Another favourite was the poem on *'Old Rothwell'* written by John Sykes, 'The Blind Poet', who had died here in 1869 aged only 29. Later it was set to music by C. Gibson, the parish clerk, and published in the Parish Magazine in January, 1878. Local history was another interest, Charles' mother being a ready source of information back into the 1830s. For the earlier periods, he could also contact his friend John Batty's comprehensive *History of Rothwell* which he purchased on its publication in 1877. He also displayed an interest in popular science of the period, buying Professor R.B.D. Wells' book on phrenology, the now discredited study of the shape of the skull as an indicator of the character of an individual. This was accompanied by a glazed white earthenware bust, each part of the cranium labelled with its particular significance such as 'Spirituality', 'Friendship' or 'Tune'.

As in almost every personal library of this period, he also owned good editions of the King James Bible, the Prayer Book and John Bunian's *Pilgrim's Progress*. Both his parents were regular attenders at Rothwell Parish Church, taking an active part in all its widespread social activities. As the Parish Magazine reported in June, 1913, his mother

> 'was one of the staunchest members of the church, having been connected with Rothwell Church all through her long life. She always declared that Rothwell Church was to her the dearest place on Earth, and she never ceased to thank God for all the blessings she had received there ... . All who come into contact with Mrs Brears were struck with her firm, strong faith and the beautiful calmness of her life. She had a calm word for all. Her memory to the very end was clear and bright and she could recount all manner of interesting things about Rothwell in bygone days.'

Charles appears to have inherited both his love of the church and his faith and calmness from her. It was largely through this that he took a youthful interest in church music, here learning not only to read music, but to play the organ. He is believed to have played the hymns for his first service around 1866, when only twelve years old. By the time he was in his mid forties he was able to become organist to the new church of St. Andrew at nearby Stourton, in the meantime developing his skills on the piano, violin and piccolo.

Other interests pursued as a young man included chess, played with both Staunton and earlier designs of boxwood pieces, and photography, especially of local historic buildings and of members of his family.

In the early-mid 1880s he probably first met a young teacher called Mary Ann Boucher when she took up her first post at the Rothwell Church/National Schools. Here, in addition to

Holy Trinity Church, Rothwell, had a fine choir of male and female voices in the mid nineteenth century. Here Charles learnt to play the organ, completing his first service when only twelve years old. His photograph, taken by Albert Scott of Leeds, is one of the earliest of the church, showing all the box-tombs which have now disappeared.

teaching, she attended the annual school concerts which had been held in the Mechanics Institute each December since 1875. As one of the highlights of the town's social calendar, each concert was extremely popular, tickets for reserved seats costing 1s (5p), front seats 6d (2.5p) and back seats 3d (1.25p). The specially-printed programmes provide an interesting insight into the popular musical tastes of the period. Proceedings always commenced with the National Anthem, perhaps followed by part songs by the Church Choir Glee Party, or Christmas carols by the scholars. For the remainder of the evening there were piano, violin, or cornet solos, or songs by gifted individuals, but choral works predominated. In addition to more carols, such as 'See amid the winter's snow', 'In the fields with their flocks abiding', and 'Emanuel' there were narrative songs including 'D'ye ken John Peel', 'The Jolly Miller', 'Four Jolly Smiths', 'Hop Pickers' or the resounding 'Farmer's Boy'. Since this was at the height of British Imperial power, there were numerous patriotic songs too; 'Might with the Right', 'The Empire Flag', 'The Tight Little Island', 'To the tap of the Drum', the martial 'Boys of the Old Brigade' and stirring strains of 'The Minstrel Boy'. Today virtually all of these are long-forgotten, but for anyone who has experienced the magnificence of a traditional West Riding choir, it is easy to imagine their lines echoing through the dark streets of mid-winter Rothwell.

By May, 1885 Charles and Mary Anne had become sufficiently close for him to write out paragraphs on religion and Sykes' *Old Rothwell* poem in her album, using pink and purple inks. There then followed a few years of courting, or, as it was called, 'walking out together'. This, in Rothwell, involved strolling together along Park Lane or the more secluded Methley Lane, locally known as 'The Duck Walk'.

Sometimes Charles and Mary Anne would take a recreational walk from Rothwell out to Cheesecake House, not far from Iveridge Hall, on the east side of the Wakefield Road, then little more than a pleasant leafy lane. The House was a rare survival of the once common form of single-storey timber-framed cottage, with two rooms at ground level, and three in the loft, these being accessed by a spiral staircase with steps made from blocks of oak. It was occupied by Matthew (better known as 'Mather') Brook, a self-employed joiner and cabinet maker, who had his workshop there. Slowly the demand for his work fell off due to the expansion of the Leeds furniture industry. Fortunately he then became a foreman at a boatyard making barges for the Aire and Calder Navigation at Castleford. Apparently he had come across two men discussing their problems in building a new kind of barge, joined in their conversation, worked out a bill of quantities and an estimate for the project, and was then given the contract. At the launch, the chairman told him that he had undercut the nearest tender by some £200, and rewarded him with the post of foreman.

The couple's visits to Cheesecake House were not concerned

with woodwork, however, but to take tea. Mather's wife, Mary, kept two nanny and one billy goat, converting the milk into curds which she then mixed with eggs, butter, sugar, currants and nutmeg to make the most delicious Yorkshire cheesecakes of various sizes. She baked both in a traditional cast-iron Yorkshire range, and in a domed masonry 'bee-hive' oven set some four feet to one side. Its base, a three-inch thick slab of stone, gave her an ideal heat with which to bake her puff pastry confectionery, such as custard-filled vanilla slices. These, with the cheesecakes, brought in numerous people on foot, in wagonettes and later in charabancs to take tea and snacks in the garden, or in the house when there was bad weather.

Mary Anne's family lived at Ripley, the Ingleby family's estate village just north of Harrogate. Here too the couple walked the numerous rural footpaths together, studying and collecting samples of the local flora. On their autumnal walks, they also collected some two hundred small, dark hazelnuts. These were for neither study nor eating, however, but to serve as counters for the game of put-and-take. For this, her father made a teetotem in the form of a short eight-sided roller, the faces being marked in ink ALL, PIII, TII, TIII, NONE, TI, PII and PI. From time to time over the next eighty years, when they, their children, grandchildren and great grand-child sat around the cloth-covered kitchen table in an evening, the bag of nuts and the teetotem would be brought out and tipped into a heap in the middle. Everyone then drew out a selected number of nuts, perhaps a dozen or twenty, depending on the number of players, but always leaving about a half or third in the centre. The teetotem was then passed around the table, each person in turn rolling it along the cloth to reveal the random 'ALL', 'P...', 'T...', or 'NONE'. If a PII or TIII turned up, they would put two nuts, or take three nuts from the central pile, or do nothing if they got 'NONE'. So it continued until one person had won all the nuts. This could take forever, especially when someone got 'ALL', and took the central pile for themselves. It was a game of no skill, but enabled the family to pass a long winter evening in an easy communal way, children and adults competing on equal terms.

Charles and Mary Anne were married at Ripley Parish Church on 3rd August, 1888. The register recorded their ages as 33 and 26 respectively, and that her parents John and Elizabeth were the official witnesses. Charles had by now left the mines to work as a draper's assistant in a central Leeds shop. This would certainly reduce his income, but also decrease his risk of severe injury, death or premature incapacity through occupational complaints. Only those brought up in a mining community can really appreciate the risks involved, or the reasons why so many miners hoped that their sons would never have to follow them down the pit.

Charles married Mary Anne Boucher at Ripley Parish Church in August 1888. This drawing of the church was made about the same time by her father, John Boucher.

Presumably the wedding was followed by a celebration across the market square in the Star Inn (now the Boar's Head). There are no records of any presents, except for a slim copy of F.E. Weatherly's poem 'The Honeymoon' from Mary Anne's sister Lizzie.

Wife and In-Laws

In the 1840s the Boucher family were farmers at Hampsthwaite in Nidderdale. Richard Boucher's son John trained as a joiner, his work probably bringing him into contact with Thomas Atkinson, blacksmith in the village of Killinghall in the same parish. On 15th April, 1854, 29-year-old John married Thomas' daughter, the 24-year-old Hannah Atkinson, at Ripley Parish Church. To celebrate the event, Thomas forged the iron fork and brass shaft of a toasting fork, John then supplying the wooden handle.

At this time John was estate joiner for the Ingleby family of Ripley Castle. They provided the couple with a house towards the south end of their neo-Tudor model village. To furnish it, John purchased planks of mahogany etc., and employed his cabinet-making skills to make everything required to furnish its

Charles, right, with his in-laws on a favourite footpath at Ripley in May 1905. John Boucher stands to the left, and Mary Anne, Charles' wife, between her sisters Ellen and Lizzie.

main rooms. He already had a fly table in oak and elm, its legs elegantly turned in the most fashionable style, which he had made at the completion of his apprenticeship in 1842. To this he now added a mahogany bureau-bookcase, its glazed doors given flat, Tudor arches to match those of the windows in his house. There was also a circular tripod-based dining table, a small side-table or 'stand', an ingenious sofa, the seat of which concealed an extending teak-framed double bed, and a set of hanging shelves. The living room also had an older oak corner cupboard, its door inlaid with a shell motif in veneers. Before it was screwed to the wall, its back was covered with a copy of the *Leeds Mercury*, carrying reports of the British Army in the Crimea, subscriptions to the Patriotic Fund, and local news from Bradford, Huddersfield, Wakefield, Halifax, Dewsbury and Settle. Inside, its bottle-green painted shelves were filled with a selection of Bristol Blue glasses and bowls, some with gilt decoration, along with copper lustre jugs and mugs with brightly-coloured bands of floral decoration. Here too was a fine china tea service made by William Hilditch & Sons at Lane End Pottery, Stoke on Trent, around 1825-1830, its decoration being roses and sprays of crimson and purple brushwork. This was probably inherited from his father.

For the bedrooms he made a fine mahogany bow-fronted chest of drawers, but bought a pine bed, wash-stand and chest of drawers grained to resemble pale bird's-eye maple. This was identical to those made by R. Railton, cabinet maker of Northallerton, and may perhaps have been made by that firm.

During his long working life, John Boucher undertook all manner of woodwork for the estate and the castle. In the Knight's Chamber, for example, he had been inside the priest's hole concealed behind the wainscot panelling near the staircase, believing that this would enable an escaping fugitive to descend and leave by the drain-cum-tunnel near the base of the tower. Other work included everything from repairs to properties on the estate, making gates etc., or constructing complete roofs for barns etc. Later tasks included building one of the first generation of poultry battery houses, bringing numerous enquiries from fellow villagers – his response being that Ingleby's were such a caring family that they had ordered him to build a convalescent home for consumptive turkeys!

He was always extremely fit, being an accomplished Dales step-dancer and a figure skater, one of his annual tasks being to test the strength of the ice on the Castle's lake before it was allowed to be used by others. His enforced retirement at the age of around 80 was, in his opinion, totally unjustified, and so

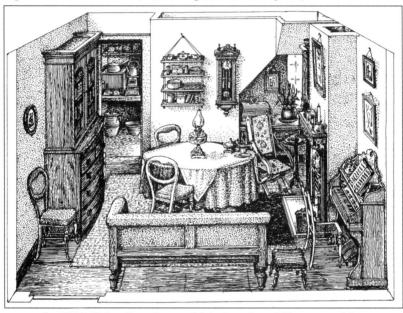

In 1903 John Boucher and his daughter Ellen moved into this tiny estate cottage at Ripley, taking with them the chest of drawers, top of the bureau bookcase, fly table etc. he had made almost fifty years before. When Charles and his wife came to stay, the top of the central table was tipped up vertically, and the sofa, specially made by John, folded out to make a double bed. Since there was only a side-boiler and a chimney crane over the fire, all food had to be cooked in the back lobby-cum-larder-cum kitchen, where there was a cold tap, a small sink, a paraffin stove and a paraffin oven.

he marked his last day by walking along the high ridge-tree of a barn roof he had just completed, and spending the evening step-dancing in the Star.

By this time he was using a tricycle instead of walking for long distances, but found it hard work to pedal up the steep hills. Since his arms were as strong as ever, he got the village blacksmith to mount a hand-turned sprocket wheel on the side of the steering column, from which a loop of chain passed round another sprocket on the back axle. In trials, this device appeared to work extremely well, and so he decided to give it a public demonstration the following Sunday. As the remainder of the congregation chatted in the market square after church, he mounted his tryke, and approached at maximum speed. Suddenly something went wrong, he lost control and charged the open door of the Star, which he would have entered, had it not been for the width of the back wheels. He was then forced to dismount and wheel the tryke back to the blacksmith's shop, a subject of great amusement to all the spectators. He was so embarrassed that he avoided church for the next few weeks.

John and Hannah had three daughters;

Mary Anne (31/12/1861 – 8/4/1927), who married Charles Brears

Elizabeth (12/11/1865 – c. 1950), who married William Porter and spent her life in Jersey.

Ellen (?/2/1870 – 17/11/1954), who lived all her life at Ripley.

As children they all played with a prettily painted Noah's ark with dozens of pairs of animals, and learned needlework skills from their mother. Her major sampler, featuring Adam and Eve, birds and decorated borders, hung in a dark-painted frame over the fireplace, complete with embroidered inscription 'Hanna Atkinson work ended April 27 in year of our Lord 1842 aged 11 years.' The girls made their own sequence of samplers while attending Killinghall school. Elizabeth's are dated to 1878-

9, and 1881, featuring her name and alphabets. Ellen's eight samplers are similar, being made when she was 8, 9, 10 and 12 years. When 11 she completed a larger example taking the form of 'Palestine in the Time of our Saviour Ellen Boucher, Killinghall School, 1881.' Her father mounted this in a reeded oak frame, and hung it in the living room.

As estate joiner, John Boucher built this innovative poultry battery-house at Ripley in 1905.

Like many of their contemporaries, the girls joined the Band of Hope and Temperance Society, which aimed to turn children away from the demon drink, alcohol. On Whit-Tuesday, May 18th, 1880, they attended the Society's demonstration at Killinghall, singing teetotal hymns such as 'The Little Newsboy', 'Dear Old Home', 'Sound the Battle Cry', 'Vote it out', 'The temperance Army' and

> 'Hurrah, for sparkling water,
> The cool, the pure, and free;
> The silver plashing water,
> That murmurs o'er the lea;

It gives us health and vigour,
It makes us bold and strong;
Unfurl the temp'rance banner,
And this shall be our song:

CHORUS, -
Hurrah! Hurrah!
Hurrah for sparkling water,
Hurrah,hurrah for water,
The cool, the pure, and free.

They also wrote out temperance poems on sheets of writing paper, these including 'The Teetotal Mill' and 'The lips that touch Liquor shall Never touch Mine.'

Mary Anne always had an interest in natural history. In January 1877 her 'Prize for good conduct & regular attendance at Killinghall Sunday School' was a copy of W.S. Coleman's *Our Woodlands, Heaths and Hedges,* describing every native tree and shrub in text, woodcut and some colour illustrations. After leaving school she went on to study at the Ripon, Wakefield and Bradford Training College in College Road, Ripon. Built in 1858-9, it trained teachers for posts in Church of England schools. Here too she developed her study of natural history, receiving the Rev. C.A. John's *Flowers of the Field* 'With love and best wishes of her College Friends' for her 24th birthday in December 1885. This had over six hundred pages of descriptions of all native plants, her copy still including pressed specimens interleaved in their appropriate places.

Her own collection of 110 pressed wild flowers were mounted in two exercise books, within elegantly engraved coloured card covers. That from the Northern Educational Trading Company of York and Leeds featured views of York Minster, Leeds Town Hall, Scarborough Castle and Haweswater. Each specimen was given its traditional English name, followed by its botanical name, and sometimes its provenance such as 'Ripley Wood June 1881', 'Clint July 1882' or 'Caton Gill Aug 1882'. She also developed a fine collection of birds-eggs, for which her father made a case with numerous compartments, each with its egg, padded base and name-card.

In 1883, her last year at College, Mary Anne purchased a morocco-bound album, its blank pages being of different pastel shades. Its purpose was to allow each friend to decorate and inscribe each page so that, as she wrote at the beginning;

> 'Some token I beg may appear
> I'll leave for your taste to select
> The subject in poem or prose
> But trust you will not neglect
> To copy something or compose
> Then when far away from my view
> Mementos you've left me behind
> Will help me to think oft of you
> And friendship more firmly will bind'

All are penned in the neatest of copperplate scripts, sometimes within floral borders and enriched with penwork or watercolour. One sheet of 'The Cards of my College Friends 1882-3' gives their names and addresses, most coming from Yorkshire and Lancashire, along with others from Northants, Herts, Staffs and Durham. Entries continued to be made in later years, one by her father having a view of 'Ripley Church, Yorkshire' and a verse entitled 'Fear God'.

For the five years after leaving College Mary Anne taught at Rothwell Church Schools. On marrying, however, she gave this up to become a full-time housewife, as was to be expected at that time.

Setting Up

Charles and Mary Anne's first home was at 7 Beech Grove, Stourton, but around 1898-9 they moved a short distance to No. 3 Pontefract Road, taking over the bakery and confectionery business of William Branson. By 1900 they had expanded into No. 4, which now became the Stourton sub-post-office. Abandoning her teaching skills, Mary Anne now became a full-time baker and confectioner. Among her most popular products were apple, plum, or other soft-fruit pies, double-crusted and baked in nine-inch buff stoneware dishes, each stamped 'GUARANTEED/ FIRE PROOF/MADE IN ENGLAND', one of which I still use today, after 110 years continuous use. Local carriers bought either a whole one, a half or a quarter, as they passed by. She also made bread and a range of cakes.

Next door Charles ran the post office. Every morning a horse-drawn post-office van driven by Charlie Robinson set off from the central sorting office in Leeds, collecting mail from a postbox in Hunslet and from Stourton post office at 8a.m. He then went to collect from Oulton and Methley, rested the horse for an hour behind the Royal Oak on Methley Lane, before returning to Leeds via Rothwell, Rothwell Haigh, Bell Hill, Stourton and Hunslet. The horse knew the route intimately, stopping at each box in turn, and refusing to move on until it heard the postman open, close and re-lock its iron door. Any attempt to miss a box caused it to dig its heels in, turn its head round, and listen for the expected sounds, since it was stone blind. These regular habits caused problems when the post office was transferred from the Gillings' to the Brears' shop. The horse always went on to its former stop, then having to be turned round and tempted back with lumps of sugar. It was an excellent timekeeper, only failing once – just outside the lodge of the Earl of Mexborough's Methley Park it trod on a broken bottle, could not be saved, and so bled to death there.

As the shop and bakehouse occupied the ground floor, the

main living room was on the first floor, adjacent to the bedrooms. There is hardly any information from which to reconstruct the decoration and furnishing of ordinary living rooms in late Victorian and Edwardian Leeds, but it is possible to do so for that of Charles and Mary Anne. The reasons for this are twofold; firstly Charles took photographs of its interior, and secondly, I grew up using most of its furniture, which was only sold in the late 1970s.

There are virtually no photographs recording the interiors of ordinary homes in Victorian Leeds. Charles' photographs of he and his wife in the parlour over their shop at 3, Pontefract Road, Stourton, are therefore of great interest.

As the photos show, it was a high-ceilinged room, the floral print wallpaper extending from skirting board to cornice, with no dado, picture-rail or frieze. The woodwork was painted in two colours, the skirting boards, door surrounds and door panels in a darker tone, the door frames in one much lighter. The entire floor was then covered in an oil-cloth or linoleum, its central area having a carpet square with an all-over scroll and flower design.

In front of the fender, with its turned finials, was a rectangular hearthrug with long black hair, probably made of goatskin. Such rugs caught much of the dust from the coal fire, and could be shaken outside, while their colour disguised any scorching caused by escaping sparks or embers.

The centre of the room was occupied by a round mahogany tripod table, usually covered with a dark bobble-edged chenille cloth, embroidered with sprays of large flowers. On it stood a fine brass 'Duplex' oil lamp, double-wicked to give an excellent light. There was also an octagonal workbox table, its inlaid chessboard top lifting to reveal rich red silk-lined compartments, each with its padded and covered lid, the whole tapering to a tripod base. Around these were arranged mahogany easy and side chairs, and a sofa beneath the windows.

The main formal arrangement of furniture lay against the inner wall. This centred on a mahogany dresser base, its top drawer holding sheet music and small musical instruments, more accompanying the violin on the shelf and drawer behind the double doors. Here too Charles probably stored his magic lantern with its sets of coloured slides of pantomimes, military expeditions, circus scenes etc., and his camera equipment. The mahogany bookcase above held all Charles and Mary Anne's books, a framed photo of Durham Cathedral standing on a miniature easel in front, with plaster busts of Bach and Beethoven to each side. A portrait of Queen Victoria occupied the wallspace above, with others of Mr. Gladstone and probably another politician hung in Oxford frames to each side. These, together with a piano, a pedimented slate clock on the mantelpiece, a potted plant in a jardiniere, and a stuffed stoat and squirrel, completed the furnishings of this room.

The main bedroom, meanwhile, had an iron-framed bed, the usual alternative to wood-framed beds which could conceal bed-bugs. To accompany it, the wardrobe, wash-hand stand, three-drawer chest of drawers and swivelling mirror on stand were all made of ash, each piece being finished with reeded bands and a hard-wearing clear varnish.

*Using their combined incomes Charles and Mary Anne were able
to provide themselves with comfortable furnishings. These included
a varnished ash bedroom suite (top), a set of mahogany chairs
upholstered in dark red velvet, and a mahogany bookcase and table.
His interests were represented by the chess-table, violin, piano, busts
of composers and for phrenology, and the marble clock, presented
by his choir. The stuffed squirrel and potted plants showed her
continuing interest in natural history.*

Since none of these pieces had been inherited or given to Charles and Mary Anne, they demonstrate that their first years together had proved very successful. As their photos show, they could afford to dress in the height of fashion. Even as a small businessman, Charles now appeared in a silk-faced frock coat, stiff collar and top hat, his wife in fine blouses, black-laced short capes and silver mounted umbrella.

Charles' photograph of St. Andrew's Parish Church, Stourton, where he served as organist and choirmaster. Following the decision to destroy the whole village of Stourton, it was demolished in the mid-late twentieth century.

While at Pontefract Road, construction started on the first Church of England church in Stourton, its site being only a short distance from their house. Dedicated to St. Andrew, it opened for services in 1898, with Charles as its first organist. A photo of the choir taken in 1899 show that it had a 15-strong male section, 17 boys and 8 ladies. Along with these duties, Charles also became treasurer of the local branch of the Good Shepherds friendly society, a provider of security and assistance especially important before the introduction of the National Health Service and unemployment benefit. He stored the subscriptions in a small polished oak box, its lid secured by three separate locks, so that it could only be opened in the presence of three designated officers. For ceremonial occasions, this office gave him the use of a symbolic shepherd's crook, its brass head being mounted on

The Choir of St. Andrew's Parish Church, Stourton, 1899.
<u>Back Row</u>: Mr. Roberts. Abraham Smith. George Gill. Arthur Radford. Charles Brears (organist). Mr. Warwick. Bert Duff
<u>Second Row</u>: Harry Duffill. George Forman. Fred Ellison. James Gouldthorpe. Richard Gill. Rev. G.H. Clark. Robert Tetley. Willie Idle. Tom Vickers. Henry Sheldon. 11. George Burgess.
<u>Third Row</u>: Selwyn Wade. George Stephenson. Mary Westerman. Miss Gill. Miss Ellison. Miss Gill. Miss Blackburn. Miss Gibson. GeorgeTodd. Walter Atack.
<u>Front Row</u>: Alfred Scott. Addison Barber. Walter Scott. Arthur Todd. Harry Sheldon. Fred Duffill. Claude Burgess. David Brears. Sydney Ely. Major Sheldon. Bert Warwick. Albert Cockayne.

a finely-turned and polished ebony shaft.

The 1880s and 90s had seen Charles' life progress in every direction, for he had left the pit, set up his own business, married well, and had taken up useful positions in his local society. In addition, he and Mary now had two young sons.

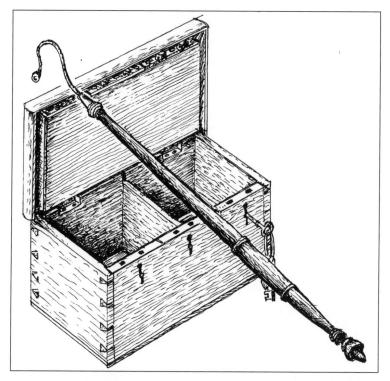

As treasurer of the Good Shepherds' friendly society Charles carried this ceremonial staff in the form of a shepherds' crook. The oak box, made by his father-in-law, had three locks, so that it could only be opened when all the chief officers were present.

Sons

Charles and Mary Anne's first child, a son, was born at 9.15 a.m. on 7th July 1889, and baptised at Rothwell Parish Church two weeks later, on the 22nd. As was usual at this time, he was given his mother's surname as one of his Christian names, being christened Edward Boucher Brears. To celebrate the event, firstly a christening mug of bone china was commissioned from one of the city-centre shops, his name being applied in a gilded copperplate script. Secondly, his parents went out and bought an enormous morocco-boarded, brass-bound and brass-clasped family bible, complete with numerous colour plates and pages ready to receive 'Parents Names', 'Children's Names' etc., which they proceeded to fill in.

A second son arrived at 1.30a.m. on 5th January 1892, when the family were still on holiday with their Brears and Jackson sisters in Muncaster. After a rapid return home, his birth was registered as having happened at 7, Beech Grove, Stourton. In some families it was still important that sons should be registered in Yorkshire, in order that they might eventually be eligible to play for the county cricket team. This was not the case here, however. Under the Poor Laws, individuals had only been able to obtain relief from the Poor Law Union in which they had been born, and so it was important for births to be registered in one's own locality, even if the actual events took place a considerable distance away. Like his elder brother, this second son was baptised at Rothwell Parish Church, where he was christened David John after his two grandfathers.

Since Charles had worked as a drapers' assistant in Leeds, he made sure that both of his children were well-dressed. Towards the end of 1892 he had their photograph taken by C.E. Spencer of 61 New Briggate. David, being a one-year old, was still in a dark frock with a lace collar and lace smock, while three-year old Edward was already in knickerbockers, stockings and boots, complete with a lace-collared military-style tunic, a crown and

.As a draper, Charles made sure that his children were always well-dressed. Here, clockwise from the top, are David and his three-year old brother Edward in 1893, and David aged about four, about six, and a few years older as a choirboy at St. Andrew's Church.

sergeants' stripes embroidered on the sleeve. At this time there can have been no preconception about what was to happen over the next few months. In the spring of 1892 a diphtheria epidemic had started to spread throughout the country. This highly infectious bacillus attacked the membranes of the throat, frequently proving fatal, especially to children. Edward caught it a few months before his fourth birthday. Despite being rushed to the Leeds General Infirmary, he died there at 6.55a.m. on 27th April, 1893, then being buried a few days later in the churchyard at Rothwell. As there were to be no other children, David was now brought up as an only son.

Commissioned to celebrate the birth of their first-born, the china mug on the left rapidly turned into Edward's memorial after he died from diphtheria when only three years old. The central mug, given to his brother David, had a whistle in the bird's tail, while the third was a souvenir of a visit to Fountains Abbey.

A photograph taken by Hartley Baron of 14 New Briggate shows him at around four years old wearing a lace-collared knickerbocker suit and posing with a bat and ball. Later photos by Francis Scrimshaw 'A little below Marsden's Monument, 28 Woodhouse Lane, Leeds' see him at about five in a lace-collared knickerbocker suit of hard-wearing tweed, with ribbed stockings and stout steel-tipped boots, very practical wear for going to school and playing around the cobbled streets of Stourton.

Although Stourton was administratively in Rothwell, it was for most practical purposes an outer suburb of Leeds, occupying the junction between the main roads from Castleford and Pontefract, and from Wakefield, with Low Road, the main route into the city through the great Hunslet engineering factories. For a small boy, it was a fascinating area in which to grow up, for there were so many different things and places to be seen and explored. Cartloads of rags were always arriving here to be sorted for the paper mill, for example, the rag-sorters being obliged to live in the owner's L-shaped terrace of cottages called 'Brown's Buildings'. White cotton and linen were best for white papers, while indigo-died butchers aprons etc. provided useful blue colouring for pale blue writing papers. Once sorted, the rags were torn to shreds in a 'devil', a machine with hundreds of claw-like steel teeth rotating on a high-speed drum. The mill also made brown papers used for wrapping and paper bags.

Although major factories such as Coghlan's Forge did not allow children to enter, other workshops might be far more tolerant. When watching local blacksmiths at work, they were frequently told to 'Bugger off, ye little buggers!', but at Tommy's forge, down a side-passage, they were usually allowed to watch him shoeing horses, tyring wheels etc. The cobbler's shop was a timber-framed and boarded shop-fronted hut standing at the Stourton end of Thwaite Lane. (I remember it still being there in the 1960s). Here, on winter nights, when it was too cold and dark to play out in the streets, all the boys used to congregate around the cobbler's glowing pot-bellied iron stove, chatting and entertaining themselves as he continued with his work. The cobbler here was an old soldier, who had served in the Crimean War of the 1850s. While under fire from the Russians, he had noticed a spent cannon ball rolling along the ground towards him. Without thinking, he put out his foot to stop it like a football – with the result that he received a serious injury which left him with a limp for the rest of his life.

Another place to visit was Thwaite Mills. Here he saw the enormous waterwheels powering the crushing, grinding and mixing machinery which converted chalk into whiting for whitewashing ceilings and cellars, putty for windows, or Paris White. This was a

Since David shared a school-desk with one of the Horn's daughters, he was always made welcome at Thwaite Mills, being impressed by the huge water-wheels and grinding machinery.

very fine whiting used for polishing and similar industrial processes. He was made particularly welcome here, since he shared a two-seater iron-framed desk at school with one of the daughters of the Horne family who operated the mills.

Other experiences of working life were gained from regular visits to his grandfather, who continued as a shoemaker in Rothwell up to his death in 1900. Even though under eight, David helped in his workshop, becoming adept at making 'waxed ends', fixing a pig-bristle to the end of each thread so that it could pass through the stitch-holes in each piece of leather. This and other skills enabled him to repair his family's shoes with some of his grandfather's tools, right through to the 1960s.

The lanes and fields around late Victorian and Edwardian Stourton also offered plenty of space for recreation. Here David could gather nettles, dandelions and burdock for flavouring home-made beers and drinks. He also plucked off and nibbled the tender young leaves of hawthorn every spring. These were always known as 'bread-and-cheese', popular childhood fare. One of the major local crops was forced rhubarb. This method of growing delicate long, thin pink stalks was already well known

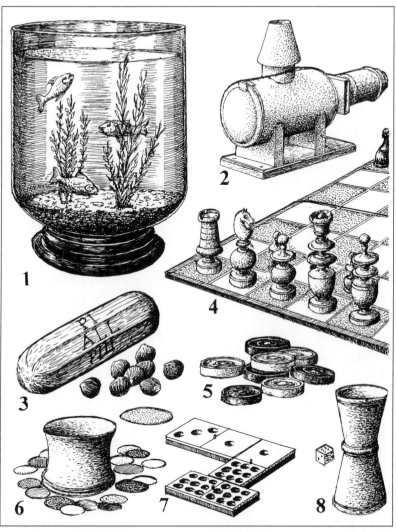

In the years before television most homes had a range of games etc.
which helped to pass the time, especially on dark winter evenings.
Those in Charles' home included goldfish (1), a candle-powered
magic lantern (2), put and take (3), chess (4), draughts (5), tiddly-
winks (6), 'nines' dominoes (7), and a dice and dice box (8), for
various board games.

by the 1890s, but there was a strong local belief that it had first started here. It was stated that once, having planted a field of rhubarb between Queen Street and the railway, Mr. Wade found that he had fifty roots to spare. These he stored in Mr. Northen's loft behind the Old Red Lion, which he rented at 3d a week until the next spring. By being kept in the dark, and warmed by the heat of the horses in the stabling below, the roots were later found to have sent out their typical forced-rhubarb stalks. Seizing this opportunity, Mr. Wade secretly harvested his unexpected crop, took it to London, sold it at Covent Garden, and then returned to Stourton to build the first-ever forcing sheds on the Queen Street site. This, at least, is the traditional Stourton version of the origin of the local forced rhubarb trade.

David also had clear memories of specific events around this period. The earliest of these was one evening in June, 1895, when he was only three. News had arrived that the beautiful Leeds Central Market at the junction of Duncan Street and New Market Street had caught fire. His father then took him to see the blaze, carrying him high on his shoulders so that he could enjoy a good view.

Other memories centred around the Boer War, when he and other patriotic local children marched around like soldiers while singing;

> 'Vote, vote, vote for Baden Powell,
> He'll help Britain to win the war.
> If thi Father is a Boer,
> Then we'll kick him out o't door
> And tha'll niver see thi Father any moor!'

or;

> 'Lord Roberts and Kitchener,
> Baden Powell and White,
> Four of the British generals
> Going out there to fight.
> And, when we get Kruger,
> Oh, how happy we'll be.
> We'll bring him over to England,
> And have a Jubilee.'

In 1900 the commander in chief, Lord Roberts, commissioned John Fowler's, the great Hunslet heavy engineering company, to manufacture four armoured road-trains. Unlike slow and vulnerable ox-carts, these trains of armour-plated wagons, pulled by a traction engine and dragging field guns, could both defend themselves, and move vast quantities of military supplies rapidly and efficiently. It took Fowlers only four months to go from initial concept through to their complete construction. Before being shipped off across to South Africa, each was driven down Low Road, and into Stourton, for efficiency trials in the Hilly Fields. As they entered the village, they stopped, the men opening the hatches and inviting the local lads, including David, to jump up inside and enjoy the ride. So off they went, shooting imaginary Boers with their elder-stalk 'rifles' for a few hours as they trundled up and down the fields.

In 1900 General Lord Roberts ordered armoured road trains for the Boer War from the great Hynslet engineering works of John Fowler. As this one passed through Stourton for trials in the 'Hilly Fields', David Brears and his young friends were invited on board to 'shoot' the enemy with their elder-branch rifles thrust out of the firing loops.

On leaving Stourton Board School in 1904, David obtained a place at the Leeds Central Higher Grade School, the huge red-brick block which still occupies Woodhouse Lane between Great George Street and Rossington Street. Opened in November 1889, it was intended to provide a three-year course offering a choice of subjects to be selected by parents and teachers, according to the child's likely future occupation. 180 scholarships were given to promising children from the borough's elementary schools, if their parents had limited means. For others, the fee was a shilling (5p) a week, or half that if, like David, he had passed 'Standard VI' at twelve years of age. The numbers taught here were enormous, 542 deaf, mute and blind children on the ground floor (where there was also a gymnasium and cookery classrooms), 752 boys on the first floor, 752 girls on the second floor, and 454 science and art students on the third floor, a daily attendance of 2,504 in the same, compact building.

The headmaster was Dr. Fothergill, who was highly respected by both the Leeds School Board and by all the pupils. On his retirement a subscription was raised to commission a fine life-sized full-length portrait of him, which hung in the school until 1993, when the pupils and teachers moved out to a new site. David remembered his teachers as being Mr. Andrews for English, maths, arithmetic and algebra, Miss Colton and Mr. Rawcliffe for French, Mr. Hutchinson for Latin, geometry and calculus, Mr. Grant for geography, Mr. Lapish for history, Mr. Pex for inorganic chemistry and Mr. Parish for organic, Dr. Pocklington for physics, Mr. Ellison and Mr. Butler for gymnasium, and a different teacher nearly every week for wood and metal work. Mr. Sutherland, meanwhile, kept the extensive stores of educational materials and books.

In March, 1983, in response to the *Yorkshire Evening Post's* request for local schoolday memories, David recorded his of seventy years earlier: 'If you were not a Leeds ratepayer, you had to take an entry examination, as only a limited number of places were available to outside pupils. If you were successful you had to pay sixpence a week school fee. The school hours were 9am to 12 noon, then 1.30 to 4.30pm. Boys and girls were educated at the same school, the girls on the upper floors (their playground was on the roof), and they entered from the Rossington Street entrance. The boys occupied the lower floors, their playground being at ground level, and they entered from Great George Street. There was the Dumb Entrance from Woodhouse Lane as well.

The boys uniform in those days had a black cap of seven panels; the front panel had a metal badge fixed, with the letters LHGS on it. Later in 1905 the cap was changed to four panels and the letters LHGS embroidered on the front. The girls wore Tam O'Shanter berets in winters and Boater straw hats in summer.

Leeds Central Higher Grade School of 1889.
The girls' playground was on the roof.

All notebooks and textbooks, lead pencils, rubbers, rulers, compasses, pens etc., had to be bought at the school. They were about half the price you had to pay in the Leeds stationery shops. There were no ball point pens in those days, and the only pen nibs we were allowed to use were the Waverley pen nibs, with the turned-up point. The large exercise book, which had to be used for homework only, had a picture of the school on the front cover.

In the classrooms we each had a separate numbered desk, and near the end of each term we had a school exam. A school report of the exam was sent to our parents, and at the next term, we had to occupy the desk in the classroom with the same number as our placings in the exam results.

There were no social activities at the school. The two main days of the year were the Annual Sport Day held in a field at Weetwood, and the Annual Prize-giving Day held in the gymnasium. The prizes were only for 100% attendance for the year. You chose your own book prize from the Leeds bookshops and submitted your choice and your name and form to the headmaster, and he purchased it to give to you at prizegiving.'

While attending the Leeds Higher Grade School, the family moved across the river Aire, leaving Stourton for No. 3 Pontefract Lane. This meant that his walks to and from school now took him through the Bank. This area of rising ground north of the river, downstream from the Parish Church, had been crammed with cheap, jerry-built housing in the early nineteenth century. By 1840 it was already seen as a dangerous area of poverty and socialism, but conditions degenerated rapidly with the arrival of hundreds of impoverished Irish families fleeing from the unspeakable horrors of the Potato Famine. Here, with little work, the poorest of diets, overcrowding, and virtually no sanitation, typhus wreaked havoc in 1847. Sixty years later little

As a schoolboy, David learned about photography both from his father and from his close friend Hubert Smith, a professional photographer for one of the leading Leeds newspapers. Here Hubert, David and his father Charles are photographing at St. John's Church, Oulton, in winter around 1906.

had changed, living conditions still being very poor, and new housing schemes many years into the future. Poverty and drink combined to produce quite a close but volatile society, in which the police virtually always patrolled in pairs. The first time David entered the area on his way from school, he was stopped by a group of men and closely questioned; who was he?, what was his name?, where did he live?, - and what was he doing there? Having given honest answers, he was allowed into the Bank, but was followed all the way back to his home. Although he was not stopped again, he was followed for the next couple of days, after which he was left to come and go as he pleased. He still had to keep his wits about him however, dodging fights, or, on one occasion, flying pokers, tongs, fire-shovels, and even a great iron kitchen fender, as they crashed out through a sash window as a domestic battle raged within.

It was always useful to have good self-defence skills. An inch-diameter ebony ledger-rule was a particularly handy piece of writing equipment to have in your pocket, for example. Even better, was a professional instructor. David therefore enrolled at 'Professor' Marks' Gymnasium which bridged the middle section of the Royal Hotel Yard between Lower Briggate and Call Lane. (I remember seeing the gym's name still painted on its wall in 1962-3, when I used to attend the weekly meeting of the Leeds Youth Mountaineering Club in the Royal Hotel). Professor Marks had been one of the first British wrestlers to have travelled to Japan to learn *ju-jitsu*. This gave him enormous advantages when entering traditional English all-in wrestling bouts. His reputation was apparently greatly enhanced when he took on the first Japanese wrestlers who came to Leeds to challenge all-comers. In contrast to all the other local wrestlers, who found themselves flying out of the ring in all directions, he was able to feign ignorance of their techniques just long enough to turn tables on them, and then achieve victory.

While he was attending school in the city centre, the whole area was subject to a phase of lavish redevelopment. This included the widening of Vicar Lane and the rebuilding of almost all its buildings, such as the City Markets and Frank Matcham's magnificent Empire Palace of Varieties and arcades, (now known as 'The Victoria Quarter'). City Square was opened in 1903, when, according to the totally apocryphal local story, Sir Thomas Brock forgot to give his statue of The Black Prince its spurs, and, on hearing the news, committed suicide. (He actually died in 1922!). Cookridge Street was widened too, involving the demolition of the old St. Anne's Cathedral, and the building of the present one on its new site, just across Great George Street from the school. The service of dedication held on 16th June, 1904 gave the schoolboys scope for typical mischief. This including the bribing of one of the workmen to release a quantity of scrap-paper punchings salvaged from nearly Chorley and Pickersgill's printing works from the ceiling at an appropriate part of the service. The addition of a little photo-sensitive solution to the holy-water stoup just within the doors had less obvious effects, until the emerging congregation began to develop brownish crosses on their foreheads as they were exposed to the daylight. Culprits were sought, perhaps even suspected, but never found.

During his time at the Central Schools, David spent most of his bank holidays with his parents on visits to his aunts and uncles at Muncaster. Other holidays he spent with his friends. One year, for example, he and three schoolmates had accommodation booked for them in a Blackpool boarding house, being sent off to the station with their rail fares to catch the train. Having met together, the boys considered their finances, and decided that they would have a much better time if they saved their fares by walking across the Pennines to their destination. They were confident of covering some thirty miles a day, and so set off, sleeping in barns overnight, to arrive two days late at their lodgings. Unfortunately they had not realised that their landlady had telegraphed their parents when they failed to arrive at the expected time, leading to severe warnings on their return. Such long-distance walks were not considered exceptional at that time. Each year a major review of all the county's regular and territorial volunteer regiments took place in York, where there were grand

Charles and David enjoyed photographing historic buildings such as Adel church and Kirkstall Abbey. Here is Charles' view of a half-timbered farmhouse at Killingbeck, not far from Cross Gates station. Unfortunately it was demolished in 1949.

marching processions to and from the Minster. These 'Military Sundays' drew crowds from a large area. David and his friends always set off in the early hours of the morning to walk to York, calling in for breakfast at the inn by the side of Micklegate Bar before going into the city.

There were frequent shorter walks too. Walking was seen as an important social pastime, something which got you out of the house in the company of family and/or friends for hours at a time, looking over the countryside and enjoying conversation. Carrying a walking stick was not a sign of infirmity, but a popular fashion for all ages. David's first cane, with a small silver band, served him in his earliest 'teens, his first smart adult cane probably being a 21st birthday present from his parents in 1913. This had a broad silver band made in Birmingham in 1912, elegantly engraved with his initials 'DJB'. Walks always featured in visits to his father's family at Muncaster, and his mother's family at Ripley. During the latter, he enjoyed his grandfather's company, benefiting from a lifetime's experience of the area's footpaths, history and natural history. A favourite route was down by the castle, across the bridge and up to the Beech Avenue which lined the track to Clint. Here, cut into the bark of one of the great trees, were his grandfather's initials, followed by his father's, then his own, these later being followed by those of his son, and eventually mine, five generations in all. Unfortunately the avenue had to be felled following one of the great gales, and no longer exists.

Other walks included Smith's farm, where back-cans were used to bring in the milk from the dairy cows in the field. It was then poured through a strainer, a 'sile', into broad, dark-glazed earthenware pans and left overnight for the cream to rise. Having been carefully skimmed off, the cream was then poured into an old-fashioned vertical plunger churn, since this was believed to produce the best butter.

On leaving school, David was taken on as a fee-paying premium pupil by George W. Slater, A.R.C.Sc., F.I.C., F.C.S., and Member of the Society of Public Analysts. This was, in essence, a professional apprenticeship in analytical chemistry and bacteriology, which ran from 14th August, 1907 to 25th August 1909. It was a very thorough and wide-ranging training. The reference he received on its completion stated that during this period at the Northern Counties Laboratories in Dock Street, besides Leeds Bridge, he had analysed, 'soaps and oils, waters for drinking and technical purposes, boiler incrustations, alloys, coal, coke, manures, foods, under the Sale of Foods and Drugs Act, and microscopical work, including the identification of the principal food starches'. He always remembered the bad quality of the food samples he had to test, ninety per cent of all the milk being found to contain the usually lethal tuberculosis bacterium for example. As a result he never afterwards consumed any milk which had not been thoroughly boiled, tea being taken black,

R. Burton, G.W. Slatter (Director), David Brears and W. Bennett, (premium pupil), in the Northern Counties Laboratory, Dock Street, in 1908. Here both chemical and biological analysis was undertaken for local authorities and various industries.

coffee only with scalded milk etc. In contrast, other parts of his training were very enjoyable, as in 1908 when he was sent to study assay work under Harry Nicholson, chief chemist at the Welsh gold mines at Dolgellau. During his two months there, Harry took him out every Saturday afternoon and Sunday, to enjoy long walks in the surrounding hill-country. So, by August 1909, he had completed his basic training and obtained a reference stating him to be 'a careful and accurate worker [who] will give satisfaction in any work'.

David's next post was still a combination of training and practical work. Since he was 18, and still a minor at that period, his contract of employment had to include his father as guarantor of its conditions. His contract with the Yorkshire Copper Works, signed on 3rd May, 1910, placed him on its staff as an analytical chemist for the next three years. In return for his services, the rights to any of his developments, his confidentiality and a good work record, he was to receive seven shillings (35p) a week for the first year, ten shillings (50p) in the second, and fifteen shillings (75p) in the third, as he became more experienced. There were also bank holidays and seven days paid leave each year.

At this time the Copper Works occupied a series of long brick workshops between Pontefract Road and the Aire and Calder Navigation, an otherwise green-field site in Stourton. The main

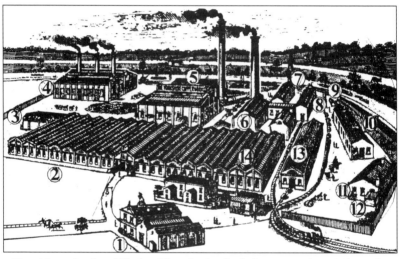

David worked as Works Chemist in the laboratory (no. 12) at the Yorkshire Copper Works in 1910-13. A world-leader in its field, the works occupied a huge site just south of the River Aire in Stourton. Its various departments comprised, clockwise from the bottom;

1. *General Office*
2. *Tank Shed for Electro-deposit*
3. *Piercing Mill*
4. *Refinery*
5. *Power House*
6. *Brass Casting Shop*
7. *Crucible Shed*
8. *Canteen*
9. *Toilets*
10. *Draughtmens' Office*
11. *Stores*
12. *Laboratory*
13. *Inspection Room*
14. *Tube Drawing Benches*

product was steam-raising boiler tubes, especially important for international naval use as the world's great powers embarked on their biggest ever arms race. Some of the tubes were made by electro-deposition in the Tank Sheds. Here David saw groups of ten black-leaded carbon mandrills revolving in tanks of copper sulphate solution, an agate burnisher regularly passing along each tube to consolidate the copper as it was deposited up to the required thickness. Most were of fairly small diameter, but one commissioned by the Japanese navy was a massive eight feet in diameter by thirty five feet long. A huge mandrill and tank had to be specially constructed to produce it, two men supervising the deposition throughout every moment of the day and night. It cost a full £2000, several millions in early 21st century values.

In 1908 Mr Gilbert Evans had left the steel tube trade to become Works Manager here, and under his direction the company also began to produce tubes by the use of rotary piercing machines. These tubes, not being of pure electrolytic copper, were much more suitable for Admiralty work. In the newly-built refinery, the copper was melted in three reverberatory furnaces before being cast into solid billets about three feet in length by men who had previously worked in the Selly Oak foundries. The billets were then tested and transferred to the piercing mill, where they passed through a Stiefel rotary piercing machine where the dies made by Mr Bob Douglas, the 'Tool Finder', formed them into tubes ranging from 1 to 10 inches in diameter.

The 'Laboratory' at that time would have been unrecognisable as such today, no gas, no electricity, and only a plumber's blowlamp to serve in place of a bunsen burner. There was, however, a fine assay balance capable of reading to 1/10,000 of a gramme. This was essential for checking the quality of the copper, zinc and tin ingots and the drilling waste mixed together to form an average sample. This was then divided into three, one part for sampling at the works, one for sampling at Leeds University and the other retained for reference. The Chilean copper contained about an ounce of gold to the ton, and David remembered that Mr Ernest Duffield, the first Secretary and Assistant Manager of the

Company, once came into the lab to discover what happened to all the gold extracted from the samples, being quite disappointed

The Yorkshire Copper Works, Staff Trip to Boston Spa, 22nd June 1910.
Back Row: Harry Davies, Head of Refinery, Dick Wright, Yard Foreman, David Brears, Works Chemist, (?), Piercing Mill Foreman, Mr. Fazackerley, Wages Clerk, Mr. Cook, Tank Shed Pump Circulatory Controller, Mr. Davies, Head of Tank Depositing Dept., Mr. Davies, Head of Turning Shed, Mr. Doxford, Head of Invoice Dept., Charles Morgan, Head of Casting Shop Mixing Dept., Herr Sponheimer, German Foreign Correspondent, (?), Hydraulic Tester, Walter Douglas, Head Tool Finder.
Middle Row: Fred Nicholson, Technical Advisor, Fred Duffield, Company Secretary, Kennth Frazer, Company General Manager, George Grenfell, Lead Burner, Gilbert Evans, Works Manager. William Walker, Storekeeper, Mr. Wood, Joiner, Mr. Foster, Head of Inspection Dept., Mr. Christiansen, European Foreign Correspondent, (?), Ledger Clerk.
Front Row: John Davies, Works Sampler, Mr. Townsend, Overseas Supervisor & Agent, Mr. Catto, Head of Power House, (?), Lathe Mechanic, (?), Office Boy, (?), Draw Bench Mechanic, (?), Tagging Machine Mechanic.

49

to discover how little came from each 5g. batch.

Further analytical and tensile testing was carried out on the finished products, this being supervised by Admiralty representatives for naval contracts. Commander Perkins usually acted for the British navy, while Engineer Commander Fujimi carried out the inspections for the Japanese. The latter selected tubes at random from batches of up to 1,000 tubes, checked them with his micrometer to the nearest ten-thousandth of an inch, and then supervised the tensile testing. On one occasion a poor tensile test on one of the tubes caused him to insist on the whole batch being scrapped immediately, and crushed in the stamping mill, regardless of protests from Mr. Evans.

At the end of his contract with the Copper Works, David moved away from home to take up the position of production and research chemist at Bradley Williams Ore Treatment Company. Their Dunston Metal Works had been set up in 1910 two miles up the Tyne from Gateshead in an industrialised dockside area. Here his job was to board the in-coming iron-ore ships, take random samples of their cargoes and analyse them before unloading. One of the first ships he boarded had a Chinese crew. As he left, the captain asked him if he had ever had a Chinese meal, a rare experience in England at that time, and so he returned later, after work. The meal was excellent, but David could not identify the meat; on asking his host what it was, they explained that it was the dog he had previously petted earlier that day, one of the chows they kept on board as a source of fresh meat!

Tyneside's riverbanks then had some notoriously violent areas. One evening, returning from work, he noticed a body floating down the river, face down with a knife stuck in the back. On reporting this to the local coroner, who lived next door to his lodgings, there was no surprise, just the question, was the body dark or light skinned? On being told it was dark he merely commented 'Oh – just "found drowned" then, explaining that there were numerous murders on board ship, always impossible to solve, and so always given this verdict. Shortly afterwards while walking along the dock, he accidentally kicked an old leather container. Instantly he found himself being viciously attacked by a raging Spanish sailor wielding an enormous dagger. Fortunately no damage was done, but it emerged that he had kicked the goatskin bag containing the sailor's personal supply of wine.

By the end of 1913 trade difficulties brought 'a temporary cessation of work' at Bradley Williams', and so he had to leave. He got a good reference from S. Evans, the manager, who confirmed that David would 'give every satisfaction' to potential future employers. His next post was as a metallurgical analyst at Moses Eden's works in Sheffield. The steel industry here was always extremely dangerous, and he remembered one man being instantly killed by white hot metal as a result of mis-directing the operator of a huge crucible. At the outbreak of the 1914-18 War, he was called in for a medical examination ready for conscription into the army. However, he was then found to have a heart defect, and was declared unfit for service. (Despite this, he never had any health problems until his late 80s and early 90s).

In 1914 David left Sheffield to work as a chemist at Brotherton & Co's tar distillery on the Cumbrian coast at Workington, not far from his relations at Muncaster. Here he lodged at 6, Old Side, until his marriage on 3rd April, 1916 with a girl he had met years before, probably through church activities back in Rothwell. She was 23 year-old Gertrude Mabel, eldest surviving daughter of Thomas Henry Bennett, builder, of 32 Carlton Lane. Like most girls of her generation, she had left school and undertaken some basic training, in her case as a milliner with her Aunt Polly in highly fashionable Chapeltown, Leeds. She had then gone into service as a lady's maid at Earlshall, Leuchars, near St. Andrews, before returning home to help her mother Elizabeth. Elizabeth had had a hard life, giving birth to eight children in twelve years, five dying when only a few months old. Worn out and toothless, she herself was to die in 1919, aged only 49.

After their marriage, David and Gertrude set up their first

home at Brick Row, Workington, where their son was born on 11th April, 1917. At his baptism he was named Charles Henry after his two grandfathers. The work at Brotherton's was both interesting and relatively well-paid, especially after he was promoted as assistant manager. He enjoyed a good reputation at the works, being 'most concencious in his work, very steady, reliable, and a good timekeeper, always willing to give a few extra hours if required. He is thoroughly conversant with Tar Distillation in all its phases, and has also had considerable experience of the manufacture of Vitriol in an intensive plant. He has had charge of the process working, and his relations with the men under him have always been satisfactory.' Clearly there was a good future here, in this major chemical company. However, early in 1920 David obtained a new and exciting post. On leaving, he was presented with a silver cake-basket finely engraved 'Presented to D.J. Brears by the Staff and Employers of Brotherton & Co. Ltd., Workington, 31st May, 1920.', and a boxed set of twelve coffee spoons and sugar tongs engraved 'B'.

The Armitage family operated major brickworks and quarries around the village of Thorpe, only a few miles away from Stourton and Rothwell. They now wished to expand into tar distillation, using the coal-tars from the nearby Robin Hood coke and gas works, and so engaged David to set up a new plant from scratch, and then manage it. This brought new status, an improved salary, one of the best houses in the village, and, most importantly, a return to their friends and relations, particularly their ageing parents. The family moved to Ashfield House, Thorpe, in the summer of 1920.

Decline

As David had been growing up and establishing his career, his parents' life had continued its well-established pattern. They still enjoyed reading, music and walks, especially during their regular visits to Mary Anne's parents in Ripley and to Charles' sister's family at Muncaster over the summer bank holidays. There were changes in their respective families, however. Charles' father died aged 82 in 1900, his mother following in 1918 aged 90, both being interred in the churchyard at Rothwell. At Ripley, Mary Anne's mother had died in 1895, her father and younger sister Ellen then moving into a smaller cottage close to the school there around 1900. There are photos of family gatherings in this cottage in 1905 and 1906, when the three sisters returned to visit their father. David, the only grandson, appears as a young teenager wearing the Eton collar and cap of the Leeds Higher Grade School. After John Boucher's death in 1910, aged 85, Ellen continued to live on in the same cottage until she died aged 84 in 1954. I can remember almost every detail of its unchanged interior, and still use some of the furniture which set up this household in 1854.

Back in Leeds, Charles and Mary Anne had also made changes to their lives. Around 1910/11 they gave up the bakehouse and post office at 3 Pontefract Road, Stourton, and moved to 67 Pontefract Lane. Despite the similarity of this new address, it was in a completely different location, on the north side of the River Aire, on the line of the medieval road between the manorial centres of Leeds and Pontefract. Lying just south of the main York road, this was a rapidly-expanding suburb of new closely-spaced terrace housing, close to the centre of the city's Irish community. Here they set up as drapers, selling ready-made clothes from the great Leeds tailoring factories, as well as cloths of all kinds. For fine magnification I still use Charles' clothier's folding magnifying glass, the square aperture in its base designed to enable the thread count of the cloth to be readily assessed.

The shop was one of a row ideally sited to meet all the needs of the local families, other traders including a milk dealer, grocer, fried fish dealer, hairdresser, glass and china dealer, greengrocer, newsagent and fishmonger. Here they made a good living for over a decade, but in the 1920s, when they were in their sixties, they decided to retire.

A few miles away, at Thorpe, their son David had been appointed to develop and manage a new chemical plant for the Armitage family, a post which brought a good salary, a spacious house and excellent prospects for the future. However, the international financial situation soon plunged the whole country into a severe depression, and all plans for the new plant were first put on hold, and then dropped. By 1923 David was out of work, with no income, but still with a wife and son to support. For months he walked into Leeds every day, roaming the streets in search of any kind of work. Even getting a day's employment skinning skate in Leeds Market was remembered as a major event. His was a common experience at that time, many highly-skilled professionals suddenly finding that their whole life's work was now of no value whatsoever, and that they had to compete for even the most basic labouring jobs. David was particularly shocked when he found one of his former instructors, a man with a doctorate and years of technical experience behind him, sweeping Boar lane with a brush and barrow, and glad of this work with the City Council. As unemployment continued, David's family just managed to get by, largely on David's wife's income as a dressmaker to the Armitages and other local families. Some relief was eventually achieved when the Armitages offered him a manual job in their Thorpe brickyard. So, in 1923, they moved out of Ashfield House into 11 Belmont Terrace, one of the adjacent terraces largely occupied by those employed in the local brick, stone-quarrying, ironworking and railway industries.

At the time, this was seen to be only a temporary setback, but, to reduce the family's overall cost of living in these different circumstances, Charles and Mary Anne decided to retire from their shop, and move in with David and his family. The arrangement worked well for a period, but only four years later, on 8th April, 1927, Mary Anne died of heart failure, aged 65.

Still believing that things must improve, the family decided to move into a larger house. New plots were being laid out along the south side of Longthorpe Lane, a short distance from the village, but offering open views across the valleys of the Aire and Calder. Since the government were offering subsidies for new-build houses, and David's father-in-law was one of the major builders in the area, he purchased a plot and commissioned F. Hartley of nearby Lofthouse to draw up the required plans. These were completed, planning permission obtained, and the mortgage agreed in July 1928, after which construction started immediately. It was a three bedroom, double-fronted detached house, at 75 Longthorpe Lane, its name 'Aysgarth' coming from a favourite area of rural Wensleydale. On completion, the family moved in, using most of the furniture which Charles had bought to set up his first home back in the late 1880s.

For a while, all was well, but the pressure of maintaining the house, the mortgage and the family in a worsening financial climate brought with it increasing stresses. Charles helped as much as he could, selling his Uncle Thomas' medals, and sawing off the silver knob of his late wife's umbrella to raise funds for food and other everyday expenses. The situation continued to build up increasing tensions within the family, however, and so, always following a happy, quiet life, he went out for a walk one day, and failed to return. David could obtain no news of his father for weeks, even months, but then discovered that he had moved into the Salvation Army lodging house in central Leeds, being reduced to living on their charity, a common experience for many of his generation. From here, he moved across to Cumbria, living with his sister Mary for the next few years.

In the mid 1930s Charles moved back to Leeds and spent some time with his son. When he was 83, he was admitted to St. George's Hospital, part of the Rothwell Workhouse, suffering from bowel cancer. When my father last saw his grandfather, he was very close to death, writhing in agony and crying out for help

After giving up the shop and using his savings to help his son and family through the financial troubles of the mid 1920s, Charles, now a widdower, went to live with his sister Mary at Muncaster in Cumbria. Here he is seen with Mary, his grandson Charles and Mary's dog Jess outside Muncaster Cottage in 1927.

from the nurses. Powerless to do anything, their only response was 'Sorry, Mr. Brears, but that's the way things are, and you'll just have to get on with it.' He died on 24th September, the death certificate stating that he had died at 75 Longthorpe Lane. This would appear to be the information his son gave to the registrar in Rothwell, rather than the actual truth, in order to avoid the workhouse connection.

Like many others, Charles had started life with few opportunities, if any, worked hard to improve himself, set up in business, married, and financed the education of his son, who went on to successfully achieve professional status. His disappointment on seeing all this swept away due to international financial disasters totally beyond his control must have been enormous. As it turned out, his son was never able to recover his position, continuing in the same heavy work of setting bricks in and out of the Thorpe brick-kilns until his retirement in 1957. However, Charles Brears' memories, photographs, records, books, musical instruments, personal items and furniture all survived him for many years, the information they retained all contributing to this study of the very ordinary life of someone who had spent almost eighty years living in various parts of South Leeds. It was nothing out of the ordinary, but for this very reason is of interest today. It clearly illustrates the experiences of many other families who were forced out of the countryside to find work in the city, benefited from its late Victorian and Edwardian prosperity, but then lost almost everything in the depression of the inter-war years.

When studying the history of any part of the country, it is relatively easy to discover details of its leading personalities, its major buildings and its most important industries. Beyond the standard sources of information, an enormous amount of fascinating and revealing detail remains in the memories of individuals and their families. Anyone who has given talks to local groups and societies soon realises that many members of his audience know more about his subject than he does, and carefully notes down their unique information. As this study shows, any ordinary working family can have memories which illuminate the past in ways totally ignored by official records. Such memories are easily lost as older people pass away, but, if possible, are always worth recording in permanent form for the benefit of future generations.